PUNishment

Dancing Sheik to Sheik

PUNishment

The Art of Punning

or

How to Lose Friends and Agonize People

Second Edition, Revised and Expanded

by Harvey C. Gordon

With a Foreword by Robert J. Herguth

Illustrations by Rand Kington

WARNER BOOKS

A Warner Communications Company

Warner Books, Inc.,
75 Rockefeller Plaza,
New York, N.Y. 10019

 A Warner Communications Company

Printed in the United States of America

First Warner Printing: April 1980

10 9 8 7 6 5 4 3 2 1

Library of Congress Cataloging in Publication Data

Gordon, Harvey C 1947–
    PUNishment: the art of punning or how to lose friends
and agonize people.

    SUMMARY: A collection of puns arranged under such
categories as "Animals," "Doctors and Dentists," "Food
and Drink," "Parts of the Body," and others. Also
discusses techniques for punsters.
    1. Puns and punning. [1. Puns and punning]
I. Kington, Rand.   II. Title.
PN6231.P8G6   1980   818'.5'407   79-23578
ISBN 0-446-97263-0

To my wife
and all my relatives, friends, and former friends
who have endured a great deal of PUNishment
over the years.

FOREWORD

by Robert J. Herguth,
Columnist, Chicago *Sun-Times*

The pun is a play on words. It is champagne to some and a champ pain to others. The word "pun," according to many dictionaries, may have come from the Italian word "puntiglio," meaning fine point. The pun is Harvey Gordon's main means of expression.

In seaside terms Harvey Gordon is a Bennett Cerf-board of America's now generation. He is a Chicago lawyer and at work he's always versus. But at home he's into verses. He decided to write this book because he's a pungent(le)man.

Some people hate puns; they are the dullards of the world, always a day late and a dullard short. Basically, they are afraid that they could never exchange pun for brilliant pun in conversation. But people with rapier wits and high I.Q.'s can be singled out instantly, because they plunk homespun puns into even the most serious chats. Puns are to words what Bach is to music, what Rembrandt is to canvas, what a French chef is to pot roast. But enough of the verbal quibbling. On to Harv and his book.

PREFACE

"We plan to pun in London, pun in Paris, pun in Stockholm and pun in Rome. You might say it will be capital PUNishment."

Harvey C. Gordon
June, 1967

I made the above statement just before embarking on my first trip to Europe after my junior year of college. My initial use of the word "PUNishment" at the time referred to clever punning which was intended to have an unforgettable impact on others.

It was during my college years that I truly began to develop my punning ability and first came into my own as a punster. It was also during those impressionable years that I started to notice the unmistakable effect punning had on other people and on my social life. Since that time, my repertoire has been greatly enlarged and my punning techniques meticulously perfected to such an extent that I can no longer keep what I know to myself, and am compelled to share my knowledge and expertise with others. The fact that I am revealing everything to the public without the use of a pun name has to demonstrate my courage—or madness.

PUNishment is dedicated to the development and recognition of the noble art of punning, the mastering of which is almost certain to cause one to lose friends and agonize people. The book contains a collection of over 400 puns that have been compiled and categorized by subject matter for easy reference. In compiling the collection, I have striven for quality rather than quantity, even though my friends, while grateful for a reduction in the latter, claim they have not noticed an appreciable improvement in the former. By familiarizing himself with this assortment of puns, a punster can establish a foundation from which he can develop his art of punning and inflict a great deal of PUNishment.

I have attempted in the second part of the book to explain the techniques of punning which I have tried to perfect over the years, and the perfection of which separates a true artist from an amateur punster. For the art of punning is much more than being able to rattle off a number of puns. In essence, it is the ability to blend clever puns smoothly into normal conversation and the ability to create puns spontaneously in appropriate situations. By applying the punning techniques to puns in the collection, a punster hopefully will begin to develop both of these abilities.

I have also included a section in the book on multilingual puns. This innovative and specialized area should be of interest to multilingual readers as well as to punsters who have developed their punning ability beyond the beginning stages (and who have access to foreign language dictionaries).

PUNishment does not address itself to the history or analysis of the use of puns in English-American literature. To my knowledge, there is no book similar in content to *PUNishment* in the sense of combining a categorical collection with suggestions on how to pun effectively. My book is intended to be extremely practical in scope in that the puns included are easily usable and adaptable, and the suggested techniques are geared to punning in everyday conversation; it is hopefully both a source book and a training manual.

In addition to trying to further the development of the art of punning, *PUNishment* is also an attempt to help obtain overdue recognition for the art. Punning has been called "the lowest form of wit." Needless to say, I disagree with this description. Most of the jokes and riddles I remember hearing or reading involve plays on words. The use of puns is considerable in television and motion picture comedy as well as in the live entertainment of theatres and nightclubs. Some of the biggest names in the field of comedy have effectively used one or more of the punning techniques discussed in this book. In short, I find puns to be the basis for a high proportion of the humor the public is exposed to in this country.

The art of punning can be a most challenging and sophisticated form of humor with tremendous opportunity for creativity and unlimited potential for getting people to laugh. It also can be a powerful weapon, as the old saying reminds us: "The pun is mightier than the sword."

TABLE OF CONTENTS

Foreword
Preface

I Categorical Collection of Puns

II Multilingual Puns

III The Art of Punning
or
How to Lose Friends and Agonize People

PUNISHMENT

I. CATEGORICAL COLLECTION

OF PUNS

1. INTRODUCTION

Webster's New World Dictionary of the American Language defines the word "pun" as "the humorous use of a word, or of words which are formed or sounded alike but have different meanings, in such a way as to play on two or more of the possible applications; a play on words." The following pages contain a group of puns which I have collected over the years and have placed in a number of convenient categories for easy reference and quick association.

In compiling my collection, I have tried to write puns in short and easily usable form for maximum applicability in ordinary conversation. There will be many times, however, when a punster will have to modify the form of a particular pun in order to fit it into a given conversation smoothly.

Some of the puns in the book are stated in dialogue form in order to express them in the smoothest possible manner and to show how they might develop in ordinary conversation. In these puns the two persons involved take the role of either the punster (P) or the unfortunate victim (V), and are so designated in the conversation.

If the reader can absorb a good number of the puns on the following pages and establish his own mental filing system, he will be ready to begin applying the suggested punning techniques discussed later in the book. I must, however, warn whoever proceeds forward from this point that my punmanship has been known to get so bad that people cannot bear to read my writing.

With this warning in mind and without further delay, it is time to turn to the first category. So, reader, open the collection. Opun!

2. ANIMALS

A relative just returned from an African safari and told us that the best way to stop an elephant from charging is to take away his credit card.

There is a rumor going around that the elephants at the circus in town are planning to go on strike. Supposedly, they are tired of working for peanuts.

A friend told me that there was a big fight in the lion house at the local zoo. Supposedly, one lion called another a cheetah. I think my friend was lion, however.

A gentleman went on an African safari exclusively to observe lions, and spent his time reading when the king of the jungle was not in sight. You might say that the man was reading between the lions.

I understand that beavers are the best dam builders in the world.

Louis (P): We saw some deer by our cabin yesterday morning.
Fred (V): Really? Did the deer have any doe?
Louis (P): Oh yes, two bucks.

(The above conversation never really took place, I just put it in for the fawn of it.)

When her favorite bull was accidentally shot, the cow rationalized the situation by thinking that to err is human, but to forgive bovine.

The cow's rationalization is food for thought, but I think nothing could be fodder from the truth.

Also, the bull's loss to the farm was not too great because he spent a lot of time sleeping. You might say he was a bulldozer.

Two silkworms were once having a race. However, they ended up in a tie.

I understand that there is a popular horse-breeding magazine in Florida that always includes a monthly center foal.

There is a superstitious jockey in California who will only ride at one racetrack. You might say the jockey has a one-track mind.

There is an animal hotel in a northwest suburb of Chicago that has an exclusive accommodation for squirrels; it is affectionately called "The Nutcracker Suite."

If I bought a farm, I would not keep a goat on the premises; I'd be afraid that someone would try to get my goat.

I would be expecially concerned if the goat had offspring; there would always be the danger of kidnapping.

I understand that a superb new breed of hunting dogs has recently been produced. The dogs have proven to be best smellers.

There is a hungry, newborn collie lost in our neighborhood who has been eating the watermelons in a neighbor's garden. He has been described as a little melancholy.

As far as I can tell, a dog's life is ruff.

The rematch race between the tortoise and the rabbit was extremely close; it was won by a hare.

A man called a veterinarian to look at his son's pony because it sounded sick. However, the vet found the pony to be all right; it was just a little hoarse.

The most vulnerable animal in the world has to be a frog because if you just touch it, it will croak.

To put it another way, one touch and a frog will be toadalled.

I always wanted to know who takes care of the potato chips in a monastery. Now I know—the chipmunks, of course.

3. ACROSS THE U.S.A.

I understand that a number of political conservatives put pages from the *New York Times* on their floors to wipe their feet on rainy days. For them the newspaper is the *Times* that dry men's soles.

The best way to drive from Dallas to Tulane University in New Orleans is to take a two-lane highway.

Legislators who favor tough marijuana laws usually feel America has gone to pot.

Reverend Brown (P): I'd like to speak to Reverend Smith in Los Angeles.
Operator (V): Is this call person to person?
Reverend Brown (P): No, it's parson to parson.
(When the operator experienced difficulty in placing the call, the Reverend told her to keep plugging away.)

There is a hotel on the near north side of Chicago called "The Carriage House," which I believe is owned by an unfortunate lady named Miss Carriage.

After the Blizzard of '79, the side streets in Chicago were in terrible shape (if you get my drift). However, there's no use worrying; with mayoral elections coming up, the streets will be cleared and you can bank on it.

You might say that senators who join a filibuster in the U.S. Senate throw their wait around.

A House-Senate conference committee considering legislation to decriminalize the use of marijuana could appropriately be described as a joint session of Congress.

I do not think a person named Patrick will ever be elected President of the United States because everyone realizes that America cannot stand pat.

The philosophy behind our federal revenue-sharing program is that spending for certain matters can be handled more efficiently at the state and city levels. In other words, one way to trim fat from federal spending is to switch to lo-cal government.

The following questions might be asked if one's mind is in a certain State.
Marsha (V): What did Tenne see?
John (P): He saw what Arkan saw.
Marsha (V): Well, what did Dela ware?
John (P): She wore a New Jersey

The state of Missouri has vigorously tried to get some of the other states bordering on the Mississippi River to join in an urgently-needed flood control project. The explanation for this action is that Missouri loves company.

The state that produces most of the pencils in the United States is Pennsylvania.

The conductors on the passenger train I took to St. Louis were very strict about enforcing the no-smoking rule in the car I was riding in; there were no butts about it.

It is said that American Indians were the first inhabitants of this country because they had reservations.

A couple in the middle of the Nevada desert drove miles and miles in every direction trying to find water, only to see that every stream they came to had dried up. "I guess we're going from one extreme to another," said one thirsty punster.

Jack (V): Where are you going on your vacation this year?
Jerry (P): Probably to California and Las Vegas.
Jack (V): Where would you stay in Vegas?
Jerry (P): We don't have the vaguest idea yet.

There are restaurants in Chicago and other cities across the country called "Trader Vic's." I heard rumors that the owners are working on a plan to open a restaurant on the moon. They plan to call it "Crater Vic's."

My brother and I took a bus tour in the San Francisco area a number of years ago. At one point in the trip the bus pulled into a rest area and the driver said, "If you look to your left, you'll see some nice summer houses; some are for men and some are for women."

When I was in San Francisco, I went to visit my friend, Mr. Chen, in Chinatown. However, somehow I got an incorrect address; I ended up at the Wong house.

After working with immigrants for a number of years, Department of Immigration officials have a tendency to become alienated.

Aside from its outstanding medical school, my alma mater, Washington University (in St. Louis), is well known for the sponge-bathing program in its nursing school. For this reason many alumni refer to the university as "old Wash U."

The 200th anniversary of the founding of each buffalo sanctuary in the United States will be marked by a Bisontennial celebration.

When some of the convicted Watergate defendants write their memoirs, they will be able to use their pen names.

I heard rumors that a girdle company is going to be the new sponsor for the TV program *Meet the Press*. Supposedly, the company is going to change the name of the program to *Press the Meat.*

You might say that the founder of Weight Watchers is living off the fat of the land.

Contrary to recent rumors the person who created the miniskirt is not a relative of former Secretary of Agriculture Earl Butz even though his name is said to be Seymour Butz.

The police raided our old fraternity house a number of months ago; its now a closed chapter, however.

The day I went on my Hawaiian vacation I left the following message with my answering service: "Here today. Gone to Maui."

The Hawaiian islands have many craters that were formed by volcanoes. You might say that the islands are full of ash holes.

A number of people go to Milwaukee to seek their fortune because they know it is the land of the big bucks. However, many eventually leave Wisconsin because they grow tired of being badgered.

When I took a trip to Minneapolis to promote *PUNishment*, I was hoping that Minnesotans would gopher my book.

4. ARTISTS AND THE ARTS

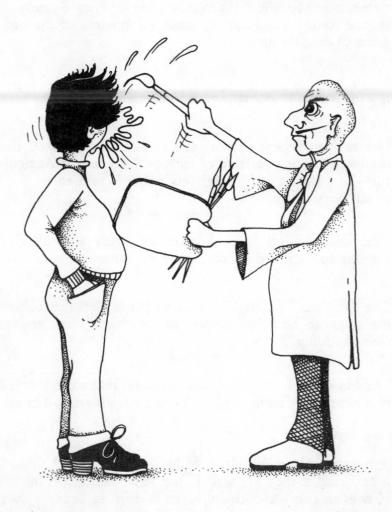

I knew an artist who carried his painting brush with him wherever he went; if he met someone he did not like, he would give them the brush.

If something happens to a work of art into which an artist has not put a great deal of time and effort, he might shrug off the loss by saying, "Easel come, easel go."

We know a husband and wife who are both artists. You might say that they are a pair of drawers.

I decided to have some of my puns illustrated because I consider myself to be an illustrious punster.

(My artist has often told me that puns make him ill(ustrate).)

A cousin of mine also used to draw. In fact, he once drew 20 years with one stroke of the pen.

A young actor was told by his agent to model in the nude for a women's magazine. The agent apparently felt the actor needed the exposure.

I have a friend who is both a mediocre actor and terribly uncoordinated. He recently fell off the stage during rehearsal and broke his leg. This is the first time he will be in the same cast for more than two weeks.

A comedian, who was just starting out in the business, told me that so far most of his fans were in his bathrooms.

A couple of ghosts entered a radio station in the middle of the night and tried to communicate with their fellow spirits around the country in what might be described as a ghost-to-ghost broadcast.

I understand that the women's liberation movement objects to the term "broadcasting" as a description for auditions for female parts in a play.

At the taping of my first TV interview one of the technicians pinned a microphone onto my suit coat. I immediately turned to the show host and said, "I thought I was doing this segment alone—not with Mike."

A movie theatre showing a film about Benjamin Franklin and the discovery of electricity might advertise the film as their current attraction.

I understand that the subject matter of the movie *Battle for the Planet of the Apes* is gorilla warfare.

The admission price to the movie *Jaws* was quite high; it cost me an arm and a leg to get in.

I heard that some theatres were charging as much as a fin.

A couple of weeks ago we heard a university drama student present an excellent reading of Edgar Allan Poe's "The Raven." People are still ravin' about it.

Many people find that jazz concerts have lots of sax appeal.

Back in 1972 I came up with the idea of writing a play about the movement to eliminate pay toilets. I have been sitting on the idea for a number of years but I feel I cannot stall any longer.

In Hawaii we saw a beautiful display of hula dancing; you might say that hula dancing is an asset to Hawaiian music.

Last Saturday night we had a great idea. We went to see the play *Dracula* and then went out for a bite.

5. BUSINESSES

Never go into the cattle-raising business. You might get a bum steer.

If that happened, you would be beefing about it for a long time.

Production costs can be very high in the dairy business. A lot of expenses are in curd.

I was told not to go into the lamp manufacturing business because I would meet a lot of shady characters.

There is a gift shop in Florida with a sign under a display of toy animals that reads: "Please do not feed the animals. They're already stuffed."

A friend told me that his parents are in the iron and steel business. His mothers irons and his father steals.

In comparison to other metal merchants, scrap dealers are among the ferrous.

I know someone who went bankrupt in the laundry business; you might say he's all washed up.

A lady walked into a florist's shop late on a Saturday afternoon only to find that all the plants in the store were off the shelves for spring cleaning. "I'm sorry, madam," the owner said, "I guess you caught us with our plants down."

Many flower shops try to carry a large assortment of plants. In other words, they try to sell every bloomin' thing.

A man in my old neighborhood is doing extremely well in the janitorial service business; he is really cleaning up.

For a garbage collecting service, business is always picking up.

Garbage collectors have a tendency to be depressed most of their working careers. They're often down in the dumps.

A record store might give a discount on a record that falls off the "Top 50" chart, and advertise it as a slipped disc.

Most fireplace shops try to sell everything the hearth desires. They usually have some grate ideas for home fireplaces.

A barbershop in our neighborhood charges $10 for a haircut; it's really a clip joint.

There is a very exclusive beauty parlor in Beverly Hills that claims to be a cut above the rest.

One of the directors of a large manufacturing company in St. Louis takes it upon himself to set up the chairs for all Board of Directors' meetings. He is unofficially known as the Chairman of the Board.

There is a businessman in Cleveland who has a reputation for excessive drinking and gambling. Members of his company unofficially refer to him as the vice president.

My aunt used to have one of the largest wig-manufacturing companies in Chicago. You might say she was once a big wig.

I understand that most tailors have alter egos.

Business for tailors is usually just sew-sew, even though some tailors seam to be doing quite well.

A man brought his badly torn pants to the scholarly Greek tailor down the street. Upon seeing the pants, the tailor asked, "Euripides?" to which the man replied, "Yes, Eumenides?"

A father brought his son into the family business with great expectations only to be greatly disappointed. Unfortunately, the day the son was told to step into his father's shoes, Dad had been wearing loafers.

Most people in the cleaning business do not believe in a free press.

Our next door neighbor, in the dry-cleaning business, lent a friend $1,000 to get started in a new business. The friend took the money and left town. You might say he took our neighbor to the cleaners.

There is a company in the area selling cemetery plots whose slogan is: "We'll be the last ones to let you down."

There is an egalitarian crematory in our city with the slogan: "All men are cremated equal."

A hotel with nice banquet facilities could advertise with a roadside sign that read: "Have Your Next Affair Here."

There is a very competitive real estate development company building homes in the subdivision down the road. Their slogan is "A lot for a little."

People in the real estate business who own or manage various types of buildings always consider roof maintenance as overhead.

A roofer who can handle all types of jobs could use the slogan: "We top 'em all."

I understand the girdle business was expanding until the bottom fell out of the market.

I have heard about a company that makes kitchen cabinets to order which claims that its workmen are professional counter fitters.

There is a provision in the lease between a regional shopping center owner and its major department store tenant calling for the former to provide a Santa Claus every year to ride on the store's escalators; this provision could be referred to as an escalator clause.

The following statement was once made at a heated bargaining session between labor and management: "We upped our offer! Up yours!"

A friend of mine who raises honey bees for a living occasionally gets stung by one of the bees. He always shrugs it off by saying, "Bee's nest is business."

Doughnut shops go out of business when they run out of dough.

I know of a swimming pool contractor who was having liquidity problems with his business. Last year, times got really bad for him, and he went under.

Many banks have special rotating doors for those customers who need a revolving line of credit.

Many pet shops keep track of their stock of miniature aquariums on their micro fiche system.

A friend of mine, who recently graduated from college, decided to go to work for a large perfume company, which makes a lot of scents.*

It turns out that this company only produces perfumes with very delicate fragrances. You might say they use the soft-smell approach.

Some retail merchants have a very specific reason for selecting a particular logo to represent their business. You might say they have a logo motive.

---

*This happens to be a triple-meaning pun.

6. DOCTORS AND DENTISTS

A medical student could not decide between psychiatry and proctology. He finally left the decision to the flip of a coin—heads or tails.

Before a doctor performs a hemorrhoid operation he embarrasses his patient.

Doctor (V): Nurse, how's the patient who swallowed a quarter?
Nurse (P): No change yet, Doctor.

After an obstetrician examined a patient who was anxious to become pregnant, the following conversation took place:
Patient (V): Well, Doctor, can I have a baby?
Doctor (P): It's conceivable.
Patient (V): You mean I can become a parent?
Doctor (P): Apparently.

The physician told his sick patient to quit smoking immediately and wanted no if's, and's or butts.

The doctor injected a number of different medications into the ailing patient, but they were all in vein.

I understand that an optometrist's greatest fear is that he will fall into his lens-grinder and make a spectacle of himself.

There are two podiatrists in my home town whom you might consider arch rivals.

There is a doctor in our town who used to be an alcoholic, but who has not touched a drop of liquor in 15 years. You might now describe him as a dry Doc.

The team doctor for the Chicago Blackhawks unfortunately is one of the funniest guys around the locker room. At one time or other he has had most of the players in stitches.

One time a player received a gash on his forehead late in the third period of an important hockey game and refused to leave the game for stitches. The angry team doctor told the player, "Suture self!"

My dermatologist is now very successful; however, he had to build his practice from scratch.

He is not like other dermatologists who promise an immediate cure for any skin disorder; that is, he does not make rash promises.

A playboy friend of mine is planning to become a surgeon because he is already quite an operator.

Under stress a good doctor does not lose his patients.

Practicing physicians in Egypt's capital city are often referred to as Cairopractors.

Doctor (V): Well, what's your problem?
Patient (P): I have a weak back.
Doctor (V): When did you get it?
Patient (P): Oh, about a week back.

My wife's cousin is one of the leading orthopedic surgeons in the country. You might say he's surgeon ahead in his field.

The oath that is hanging in my dentist's office is: "To seek the tooth, the whole tooth and nothing but the tooth, so help me God."

My dentist is thinking about going into politics because he has a lot of pull.

I understand an office with 25 dentists is opening in the big shopping center down the road. I think they are going to call their practice "Choppers World."

A dentist decided to rent some excess space in his office suite to a manicurist; however, after six months, they were fighting tooth and nail.

There are signs in many dental offices saying: "Be true to your teeth or they will be false to you."

Most dentists will not put a selection of false teeth on display in their office because they believe it's impolite to pick one's teeth in public.

Many dentists leave their practice after a short while because they find their work unpalatable.

Many ear, nose and throat specialists turn out to be ear-responsible doctors.

7. FISH AND FOWL

The last time I was fishing I ended up with a haddock. I took two aspirins immediately.

Some people only go fishing for the halibut.

I understand that fish make great brain food because they are always found in schools.

A fish recently had to leave its school because it was feeling eel.

It was no great loss, however, because its particular school was formed without porpoise.

All the musicians in the Stone Age band could play scales but no one in the group could tune a fish.

With the recent energy shortage, fish markets are trying to become more efficient by forming carp pools.

People who are forced to eat a fish diet to survive have lots of bones to pick.

A tern once graciously shared a fish it had caught with a hungry otter, and as a result of this gesture the two became quite friendly. Their friendship only illustrates the old saying that one good tern deserves an otter.

When I was in Florida I saw a sea gull land on a harbor buoy. It was clearly a case of buoy meets gull.

There is an extremely frugal acquaintance of mine whom the birds apparently know well; they talk about him constantly, "Cheep, cheep, cheep."

Turkeys are very serious-minded birds; whenever you are with them they are always talking turkey.

Right before Thanksgiving, turkeys are usually in an especially fowl mood.

Tom Turkeys that are raised on farms near China's capital city could be called "Peking toms."

Recent research has disclosed that sharks are overwhelmingly of one nationality—Finnish.

I have seen a number of apathetic owls lately; they just don't give a hoot.

I saw a superb new children's book about a peacock; it's a beautiful tale.

Two eagles took off from nearby mountain tops and nearly collided in midair. You might say the incident was a close encounter of the bird kind.

8. FOOD AND DRINK

When told by the waitress that all the restaurant had left for dessert was rice pudding, I inquired whether she was putting me on.

A fruit of the month club that includes a banana as one of its fruits has appeal.

When one melon asked another to marry it, the second replied, "Yes, but I can't elope."

If some strawberries weren't so fresh, they would not be in a jam today.

A political writer for the *Daily News* went into a popular Polynesian restaurant in the city for sweet and sour chicken. When he asked the waiter for the sweet and sour sauce recipe, the waiter replied, "Just like you journalists, we never reveal our sauce."

I hear that a number of people who plan to commit suicide drink fine wine with their last meal; supposedly, they want to digest right.

Few people are aware of all the products that are derived from a coconut. It's a lot more than it's cracked up to be.

When we go on a picnic in the woods, we like to use a special kind of preserves for our peanut butter and jelly sandwiches. The brand is called "Forest Preserves."

Customer (V): This coffee tastes like mud.
Waitress (P): That makes sense. It was ground today.

Many gourmet chefs prepare their meals with love and quiches.

A housewife left some steaks in her freezer between the ice trays. Tonight, her family will be having cube steaks for dinner.

We were invited to a party where they served a huge, thick pizza with all my favorite toppings. I never sausage a pizza.

A couple of ghosts, out for a night on the town, went into a tavern and asked the bartender if he served spirits in his establishment.

The bartender was a little annoyed, and told the ghosts to speak only when they were spooken to.

When people barbeque at a nude beach, they always make strip steaks.

My wife accuses me of burning everything I barbeque. Next weekend some friends will be coming over for filet mignon and I know my reputation will be at steak.

A toothless termite went into a tavern, crawled up to the bar and asked, "Is the bar tender here?"

I understand that Santa will have a couple of quick nips before ascending the chimney on a cold Christmas Eve. These drinks for the road might be described as his flue shots.

One New Year's Eve the Washington Capitols were losing a hockey game by four goals on their home ice and the booze came pouring from the balcony.

The following exchange took place at a well-known restaurant in Chicago:
Waiter (P): Are you ready to order, sir?
Customer (V): Do you have any spare ribs tonight?
Waiter (P): I'm sorry, sir. We sell all we make; we have no extras.

After a torrential rain had destroyed his entire lettuce crop, the farmer had his family help him replant the crop with the encouraging statement, "Lettuce begin anew."

It is obvious that the farmer is outstanding in his field.

9. FOREIGN COUNTRIES

A man sentenced to die during the French Revolution was given a choice between being burned at the stake or being guillotined. The man instantly chose the former knowing that a hot steak was better than a cold chop any time. (While the man could not keep his cool, he did not lose his head over the situation.)

I understand that executioners during the French Revolution kept track of how many chopping days there were to Christmas.

The period of European history referred to as the Dark Ages was so named because the period was full of knights.

I have heard that the World War II battlefields in Western Europe, which were littered by abandoned war equipment, were the inspiration for the great song, "Tanks for the Memories."

After a short time, the Vietnam War began to Hanoi us. Eventually, however, we decided to let Saigons be Saigons.

The first stop on our trip to Europe was Paris, where we saw all the parasites.

There was talk in Paris that if France took over the Rock of Gibraltar they would rename it "de Gaullestone."

There is a disreputable men's store in Scotland that passes off lamb's wool sweaters for cashmere. You might say they try to pull the wool over your eyes.

I understand the richest country in the world is Ireland because its capital is always Dublin.

Rome is the biggest city in the world because there are lots of places to roam.

I think Spain made a mistake when they expelled the Moors from their country in the fifteenth century. You know the old saying, "The Moor the merrier."

National Security Adviser Brzezinski and the Chairman of the Communist Party of Poland have sharply different views on many political issues; you might say they are poles apart.

To the Russians, Lenin's tomb is a special place; to Americans, it's just another Communist plot.

I understand that the pace of living is fastest in the Soviet Union; that is, wherever you turn, they're always Russian.

One day when I was touring Moscow, I discovered that all my Russian money was gone. I was left without a red cent.

An unmanned Russian spacecraft crashed onto the surface of Mars instead of making a soft landing. The Russians were unhappy because they did not planet that way.

When I suggested to my traveling companion that we economize by staying in youth hostels, he declined for fear of meeting some hostile characters.

My visit to Tehran was very hectic; wherever I went, Iran.

When we were in London, we saw a man have some exceptionally bad luck at the gambling tables. He really lost his pence.

An English punster I know told me about the times during the war when he would bring a bottle of whiskey to the air raid shelter and get bombed.

When England's economy was suffering from high inflation, government economists were consulting with Weight Watchers about getting rid of excess pounds.

I understand that in recent years the tourist business in Greece has been in ruins.

In Tel Aviv we met an Israeli who refused to touch any liquor. If I remember correctly, his name was Iva Ben Sober.

The best country in the world to buy men's neckwear in is Thailand.

When we attended the national ski championships in Norway, we saw one of the top Norwegian skiers injure himself seriously in one of the races. It was a slalom occasion.

We ended our trip in Finland where I felt most comfortable due to the fact that I spoke the language. I was told, however, that my Finnish was not very good—but neither was my beginning.

The following exchange might have taken place during the recent Egyptian-Israeli peace negotiations:
Prime Minister Begin: What will be done about our oil needs after we withdraw from the Sinai?
President Carter: Menachem, I think you're Begin the question.
President Sadat: Jimmy, our Sinai oil will be sold to all nations, including Israel.
President Carter: Anwar, I'm glad you Sadat.

Latin American terrorists are using extreme measures to eliminate their political opponents. Recently, they planted a bomb in the stomach of a bull in an attempt to kill a matador. The whole thing was abominable.

10. LAWYERS AND THE LAW

When asked if he is presently practicing law, the attorney answered that he is practicing until he gets it right.

A lawyer was attempting to collect a large sum owed to his client when he discovered the debtor had moved to Iceland, taking everything of value with him. The lawyer was then concerned about going after frozen assets.

What minority group in the United States should turn out the best lawyers? Probably Sioux Indians.

Collection attorneys are the most insecure members of the profession; they're always looking for someone to lien on.

Collecting the full amount of a judgment by garnishing the debtor's bank account might be considered a sudden debt payoff.

A friend of mine, who is an assistant state's attorney in Cook County, Illinois, was at a Chicago police station early in the morning on March 21st. When a report came over the radio about screams being heard and a man seen running with a woman's purse, my friend sighed and remarked: "It sounds like the spring's first robin."

A judge gave a TV weatherman a stiff fine for drunken driving and a warning that the next time he would be sent to jail. "Remember," the judge said, "fine today, cooler tomorrow."

For a young lawyer, a jury trial will be a trying experience.

A man recently died, leaving a large number of music boxes, pocket watches and clocks among his worldly possessions; the attorney is currently busy winding up the estate.

Regardless of the size or complexity of an estate, a good probate attorney's motto will be: "Where there's a will, there's a way."

Many attorneys carry their underwear to the laundry in their attaché cases, which is why these portfolios are often called brief cases. Also, an attorney will often carry a much smaller portfolio to court when he knows he only has a brief case.

The Consumer Fraud Division of the Attorney General's Office was investigating a large food chain for short weighting on their meat sales. Fortunately, the chain got a good report; there were no two weighs about it.

At first the U.S. Attorney's Office thought the tapes they had subpoenaed were not authentic; however, the tapes turned out to be the reel thing.

A hermit drove his 1929 jalopy into a small town, onto a sidewalk and through a store front. He was charged with recluse driving.

A successful lawyer tries not to lose his appeal.

A candidate for public office threatened to sue a certain newspaper for libel. The newspaper denied printing anything improper. When asked if he intended to press his suit, the candidate replied, "Of course; I can't campaign in wrinkled clothes."

We all feel sorry for the alcoholic lawyer who moves around the country from bar to bar.

Because I am an attorney, people often ask me the difference between "unlawful" and "illegal." My answer is quite simple: "unlawful" is something that is against the law, and "illegal" is a sick bird.

The trapped prison escapees told the sheriff's police that they would throw their hostages over the cliff; however, it was only a bluff.

A lady was brought into custody after hitting and severely injuring her husband with a three-pound canned ham during a quarrel. The woman was officially charged with attempted hamocide.

A streaker was recently pulled into court for indecent exposure; however, the state's attorney was unable to pin anything on him. (Naturally, the streaker refused to take the wrap.)

One of my classmates from law school is currently working for the Attorney General's Antitrust Division. He doesn't trust anyone.

I understand that most U.S. Attorneys prepare their cases against crooked public officials on graph paper.

There is a tavern in a small town in southern Illinois that will not sell liquor to coal mine workers; the owners are afraid of being arrested for selling liquor to minors.

The litigation attorney in our office has a special three-piece suit which he wears only in court; he calls it his law suit.

The police recently raided a massage parlor on the north side of Chicago. Apparently, a masseuse rubbed someone the wrong way.

After reading a very questionable personal injury complaint concluding with the words, "Wherefore, plaintiff prays that a judgment be entered in its favor in the amount of $1,000,000," the defendant's attorney called the plaintiff's lawyer and said, "You're going to have to pray awfully hard for that kind of money."

A notary public will always keep his seal in perfect working condition if he wants to make a good impression.

Airline hijackers appear to be respectable, law-abiding passengers when they board the plane, but turn out to be terrorists in disguise.

While some people today do not trust lawyers, it was in the days when contracts were written in stone that lawyers were really thought to be chiselers.

ESPECIALLY FOR LAWYERS

A man brought his tuxedo pants to a tailor to mend for an upcoming wedding. The tailor failed to deliver the mended pants on time, and the man had to go out and rent a tuxedo. The man sued the tailor for promise of breeches.

In a suit against a dry cleaner for alleged damage to the plaintiff's drapery, the judge was most interested in the pleadings.

Why is a covenant which runs with the land like a garter belt? I guess because it binds the assignee.

Do you know why law schools always include a section on defamation in their courses on Torts? Probably to add insult to injury.

Some of the large law schools have a special second course on Torts for those students who do not do well in the first course. I think they call it "Retorts."

I know a judge who is supposed to be a trial judge but really isn't; he just goes through the motions.

I understand that a number of judges refuse to grant summary judgments on wintery days.

What would you call a man who holds title to real property free and clear in fee simple? Most likely, a man for all seisens.

Time can pass very slowly for a young attorney who spends a good deal of his time drawing up corporate minutes, or, to put it another way, sometimes the minutes can seem like hours.

Tax lawyers are among the most thorough in the profession; they try to touch all basis.

In drawing up a contract for the purchase of a racehorse, the buyer's attorney will often add a rider.

A young attorney was being interviewed for a position with a law firm. When asked if he had a lot of experience drafting legal documents, the attorney replied, "I've done more drafting than the Selective Service office in my home town."

The senior partner in a law firm told a young associate to draw up a deed for the sale of some real estate and have it delivered to the buyer's attorney. Upon discovering that he had mistakenly given the associate some incorrect information for the deed, he inquired whether it was too late to avoid embarrassment. The associate replied, "Yes, it is; the deed is done."

While many housewives eagerly await their mail each day, lawyers eagerly await their fee mail.

11. LOVE AND MARRIAGE

I know a man who was married to a woman named Edith and having an affair with a girl named Kate. His wife found out about the affair and divorced him, which goes to show you that you can't have your Kate and Edith too.

A popular girl was going out with two guys named Ed at the same time. Her rationale was that two Eds were better than one.

Two former demonstrators from the Vietnam war era got married recently. You might say they met by chants.

There is a woman living on our block who has been married at least four times. You could describe her as a busy body. (You might also say that the woman has an altar ego.)

A short man asked a tall, well-endowed model to dance without knowing that she was married to a boxer. The man ended up getting busted in the mouth.

A young girl was anxious for Cupid to strike her heart; in other words, she was waiting for a beau and arrow.

A modern-day Cinderella was living a very lonely and tedious existence with photography as her only pleasure in life. On one occasion she took some negatives to the drugstore to be developed. After inquiring periodically for a number of weeks and finding her pictures weren't ready, she sighed and said, "Someday my prints will come."

64

At the beach a bathing beauty is considered to be a girl worth wading for.

A husband and wife were having continuous arguments about the husband's time-consuming interest in horse racing. After a while, he started getting hoarse and she became a nag.

At times my wife can be a constant complainer. One day I got fed up with her incessant grumbling and sent her home to mutter.

I think I have already given her the best ears of my life.

My wife has been very supportive and helpful with my punmanship. You might say that she's my pun kin.

Bob (P): Did you have a good time on your date last night?

Bill (V): As a matter of fact I did.

Bob (P): Who was that girl I saw you outwit?

A man from Florida came up to Chicago in January to marry his fiancée, but ended up calling off the wedding at the last minute because he got cold feet.

A smooth-talking playboy persuaded a young lady to take him back to her apartment. In the course of a philosophical discussion he asked her if she believed in the hereafter. When she responded affirmatively, he said, "Then I'll show you what I'm here after."

When at first the unpassionate playboy was unable to seduce his date, he tried a little ardor.

A teller at a local bank recently became pregnant. Apparently, her husband made the right deposit.

I know a married photographer who is in love with another woman. He would like his wife to be out of the picture.

Have you heard about the middle-aged lovers who were too tired to stay awake for a second?

I understand that many ladies carry extra slips in their purses when they go to a singles' bar. If they meet someone who gets too obnoxious, they can always give him the slip.

A young couple planned a romantic trip to Bermuda to celebrate their fifth anniversary. When asked by their parents if they were excited about their forthcoming anniversary, the couple quickly interjected. "It's our fifth coming anniversary."

There is a house in my sister's neighborhood where a family with nine children resides. Apparently, it is a house of Pill refute.

I heard about a college girl who went to a fraternity beer party, got drunk, spent the night with one of the fraters and soon after discovered she was pregnant. After her baby was born, she decided to write a book about her experience, which she chose to call *From Beer to Maternity*.

A teenager and his girlfriend were parked and making out in the front seat of his car. In the heat of passion (and much to his embarrassment) the eager lover kept bumping into the horn on his steering wheel. After the third honk, the girl said, "I didn't realize you were so horny."

12. MILITARY LIFE

I hope the army has changed its policy regarding haircuts for new recruits. To completely shave a man's head is shear nonsense.

A navy surgeon who performs hemorrhoid operations is called a rear admiral.

A dentist, who entered the army as a captain, got busted for improper conduct. His current rank is drill sergeant.

Prudent sailors don't make Waves.

One night during basic training two trainees were crawling through barbed wire with live gunfire over their heads. One trainee said to the other. "Wire we doing this?"

When I was in basic training, a punster trainee (whose identity shall not be disclosed) hung the following sign in the latrine: "Urine in the Army Now."

Many army recruits get very tired of wearing fatigues. However, they get a big kick out of boot camp.

13. OCCUPATIONS AND PROFESSIONS

Jewelers who repair watches for a living put in extremely long hours. They're always working over time.

A successful Italian mortgage banker I know calls himself "The Loan Arranger."

The most productive mortgage broker in the state of Texas might be called "The Loan Star of Texas."

A retired baker I know told me that he started out as a pilot; he used to take bread from one side of the bakery and pile it on the other.

Recently the same baker got tired of the dough and went on the loaf.

As you probably know, bakers knead to make lots of dough.

Candlemakers earn $30 per day plus an extra amount per wick.

A professional hangman was not disturbed about derogatory comments made to him about his occupation. He considered himself a practical choker.

The hangman is also one person who does not believe that no noose is good news.

A horse trainer will never have trouble getting a personal bank loan. He has a stable job.

I understand that today a lot of cobblers play sole music while they work.

I know a carpenter who tended to be undiplomatic in his dealings with other people until he fell off a ladder with a mouthful of tacks and swallowed a half dozen or so. He now might be described as a tactful person.

I was told about a young Indian who left the reservation to attend trade school and become an electrician. After gaining his union card, he decided to return home and do something for his people by installing a lighting system in the public toilet. To this day he is remembered as the first Indian to wire a head for a reservation.*

An electrician was once trying to fix a faulty circuit in an apartment building when all the lights in the entire building blew out. Unlike the building, he was not delighted.

A detective was once boasting about how great he was; he pointed to the bottom of his shoe and said; "See that heel; I ran him down."

I heard about a butcher who backed into his meat grinder and got a little behind in his work.

A surveyor who makes a plat of some land with foothills will eventually reach a plateau.

---

* Special thanks to William N. Brock of Sandusky, Ohio, for relating this story.

A well-known astronomer gave the following brief interview to a local reporter:

Reporter (V): How's business been?

Astronomer (P): It's looking up.

Reporter (V): Can you tell us anything about the UFO spotted last week?

Astronomer (P): No comet.

Accountants usually work extremely long hours during February, March and the first part of April. It is truly a taxing period for them.

I heard that old accountants never die; they just lose their balance.

I once had a cross-eyed teacher who couldn't control her pupils.

Old teachers never die; they just lose their class.

Old principals never die; they just lose their faculties.

I understand there is a minister who repeatedly straddles the fence on important social issues in his Sunday sermons. His congregation now refers to him as the Minister of Defense.

I have a friend who considers himself a band singer. His singing has been banned in a number of states.

A cheerleader for a professional football team lost her job after she appeared in a pornographic movie. Like her movie, she is now rated "Ex."

I know a photographer who frantically puts the finishing touches on his prints while his customers are in his studio to pick up their pictures; you might describe this mad rush as his photo finish.

I understand that photographers make a good living by enlarge.

A cook at the local restaurant was flipping pancakes when he lost control of a bunch in midair. The cook really blew his stack.

The folk singer considered his former music professor "instrumental" in teaching him how to play the guitar.

An attractive stewardess once overheard a conversation between a pilot and co-pilot regarding a possible strike by one of the airline unions. "Who's striking?" the stewardess inquired. "Why, you are Miss Jones," the pilot replied.

I understand that one of the major airlines will not assign a particular pilot and navigator to the same flight because the two cannot think on the same plane.

Being a geologist has to be one of the easiest professions around. If you cannot identify a particular rock, you can always take it for granite.

I know someone who cleans chimneys for a living; it soots him very well.

In addition to being highly professional, our landscaper is really a nice guy; you might say he's a very down-to-earth person.

The personnel manager of a large company interviewed five well-dressed men for the position of public relations director. The manager ended up choosing a man wearing an expensive three-piece British-tailored suit as the man best suited for the job.

Many aspiring newspaper reporters take jobs in ice cream parlors to learn how to get the scoop.

14. OIL

Oil companies are always racing against each other to find new oil reserves because they know that the oily bird gets the worm.

I know an oil driller who dug for oil in many Texas oil fields. He recently retired because he was tired of the hole business.

At a celebration party after a recent Arab oil conference the guests were dancing sheik to sheik.

The head of a wealthy Persian Gulf sheikdom refused to sell his oil to certain countries during the last war in the Mideast; however, he used his vast oil interests to induce a European lady to marry his son. The sheik believed in the old saying that "Oil is fair in love and war."

With the shortage of domestic oil, you might say that the oil exporting countries have us over a barrel.

People who drive gas-guzzling cars are being fuelish.

When we find enough oil in this country to be self-sufficient, it will be the right time to say, "Oil's well that ends well."

15. PARTS OF THE BODY

A waitress at one of my favorite restaurants has gained so much weight recently that her calves are starting to look like cows.

When my brother was overweight, people used to make jokes at his expanse.

When all the toes on my right foot were frostbitten and it was hard for me to walk, I was forced to call a toe truck.

A friend was telling me about his appendix operation when I interrupted to ask if he had a scar. He replied, "Why, no; I don't smoke."

A young lady only streaked topless across campus because a completely nude body was more than she could bare.

When chastised about her profession, the well-endowed topless dancer sadly responded, "Well, it's better than being flat busted."

(While everyone realized the dancer had a sad tale, they all agreed there was something outstanding about her.)

When I fly on a jet my ears pop and do other crazy things; it's really an earry feeling.

When a father told his long-haired son that he ought to start wearing ribbons in his hair, his son snapped back, "Quit ribbing me."

On the way to school a little boy scrambled over a barbed wire fence and tore his pants. When he arrived late, his Italian schoolteacher said: "I see you're a little behind today."

Some parents believe that swatting a naughty youngster over their knee once in a while is an important part of rearing a child.

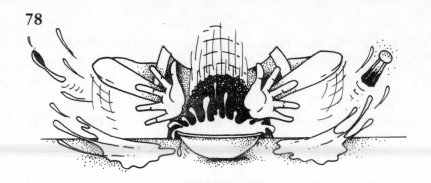

A friend of ours, Lois Lint, was complaining the other night about how often her husband sits at the dinner table with his elbows on the table and his chin between his hands. To remedy the situation I suggested that she spread a greasy substance on the table so his elbows would continually slide apart. In other words, what Lois should do is use a little elbow grease.

A mother who gives birth to twins might describe her babies as former womb mates.

A person who thinks by the yard and does by the inch should be kicked by the foot.

16. SPORTS AND RECREATIONS

A nationwide survey of college football teams has disclosed that split ends and flanker backs are usually the most unpopular players on their teams. The reason most often given for this unpopularity is, "Nobody wants you when you're down and out."

The football coach told his talented, 165-pound running back that he could not become a star unless he first became a little meteor.

A football player, who worked as a barber in the off-season, recently was forced to retire from the game. He was called too many times for clipping.

One of the players on the Tampa Bay Buccaneers bought a pair of orange earmuffs for $2 to wear during practice sessions up north. When the player asked a Detroit sportswriter what he thought of his bargain purchase, the writer replied, "Not bad for a buck an ear."

The defensive line for the Pittsburgh Steelers was quite successful in getting to the other team's quarterback last season. In fact, a couple of elated players wanted to write a book called *The Joy of Sacks*.

An attorney friend of mine, who represents professional athletes, told me that two free-agent football players came into his office and told him that they had sinus problems. When my friend looked puzzled, they explained, "No one will sign us."

This year Chicago barely won their football game with St. Louis. It just wasn't in the cards for St. Louis to win. (Chicago always considers St. Louis its Arch rival.)

The Chicago Bears once made an especially bad business deal. They paid some other NFL team a $100 waiver price and only got a quarterback.

The goalie for the Minnesota North Stars invited a young hockey fan and his dad to his house for dinner. It turned out to be quite a spiritual gathering with the father, the son and the goalie host.

Last year there was a high school football team that didn't have their game uniforms laundered all season. They were considered the most offensive team in their league.

Many basketball players spend a great deal of time observing taxidermists in order to learn how to stuff.

When I play golf, I do not land right on the green often, but I get a lot of fringe benefits.

A golfer who gets hungry when he plays 18 holes carries a sand wedge with him.

Jogging long distances can be tough on my lower legs. Sometimes after jogging six or seven miles my calves start to feel like cows.

One of my best friends in college was a champion shotputter. He could put away a shot better than anyone.

A decathlon champion might well be described as a jock of all trades.

I once met a weight lifter with awesome strength who could rip phone books like tissue paper. The man is a real terror.

In recent years there has been a tremendous surge in the number of women participating in athletics. The figures are fantastic.

A young female archer shot an arrow down range, just missing a man at one of the targets whom she did not see. You might say the man had an arrow escape.

Getting athlete's foot after losing a tough raquetball match could be described as the agony of defeat.

There are a number of tennis pros at tennis clubs across the country who have quite a racket going.

A newspaper sportswriter recently suggested that his city's major league baseball team should move to the Philippines after the team lost its pennant race by blowing a big first-place lead late in the season. He thought the team should be renamed the Manila Folders.

I understand that the White Sox do not sell beer at their ball park anymore. They lost their opener.

Two old ladies brought a bottle of gin to the ball park. When we got to the park in the fourth inning, the bags were loaded.

Many people do not realize that the Bible was the first book to refer to baseball. As you know Genesis starts with the words, "In the Big Inning."

I always bring a fish net to a baseball game because if I can catch a foul ball with it, it will be net profit.

Campers usually take afternoon rests in their sleeping bags, which is why these bags are often referred to as nap-sacks.

People who go on camping trips are usually intense people.

After traveling a short distance, a cyclist told his riding companion that he was happy the bike shop had fixed his damaged front wheel. When the wheel collapsed a short time later, and the cylist fell to the ground, his companion said, "I guess you spoke too soon."

Because of the construction of a large number of bicycle trails in our city, pedestrians and joggers have been warned to be on the lookout for cycle paths.

Two coin collectors who have known each other since youth recently got together for old dimes' sake.

Due to the high number of injuries that occur when two people ride a tandem, some communities are banning the bicycles from major streets; in effect, this amounts to a ban on cyclemates.

When a world-renowned bridge player was asked what he would do if he held the queen alone, he replied: "That depends on when the king was expected home."

When I was in competitive swimming I was once swimming a 100-yard race in a 25-yard pool. My coach, who was watching my flip turns, told me after the race that while I missed my first turn, my second turn was good and my third was even better. My response was, "Well, one good turn deserves another."

The activities director at a Colorado resort hotel knew that some of the guests were bored so he tried to stirrup some interest in horseback riding.

One should never go sailing with a haberdasher; they're always talking about cap sizes.

A woman went to a dinner party with an Olympic sprinter and told him that he looked dashing.

One night last week I went running at about midnight; I could not remember something I was going to do the next day and wanted to jog my memory.

A pregnant lady, who was a singles tennis enthusiast, decided to continue playing tennis during her pregnancy. However, she is now playing doubles.

A golfer usually will bring a third sock to the course with him in case he gets a hole in one.

17. MISCELLANEOUS

A man tried to stick his head out an empty window without realizing that his wife had replaced the glass the previous day. It turned out to be a paneful experience.

If I cannot find a partner to purchase a boat with me, I guess I'll have to float a loan.

A friend of mine, who is a great Humphrey Bogart fan, gave his wife a full-length dressing mirror·for Christmas. With the gift he enclosed a note that read: "Here's looking at you, kid."

Many people who are invited to a friend's new house for the first time bring a portable heater as a house-warming gift.

A well-known Caribbean resort recently became a nudist retreat, and the resort's apparel shop decided to have a clothes-out sale.

I know a superstitious gambler who would only play cards in men's rooms. The man apparently believes in pot luck.

A local TV news station often takes telephone polls on important political issues; you might say that the station is for whom the Bell polls.

Have you heard about the timid stone who wanted to be a little boulder?

Last year on the evening news a Chicago TV station presented a special report on the problem schoolchildren were having with head lice. After the report, one of the anchormen said, "I'm tempted to say that that was a lousy report."

A lady went into an apparel shop to buy a dress to wear for a funeral:
Lady (V): Is this a mourning dress?
Salesman (P): Oh, no, ma'am. You can wear it all day.

I have a heavy-drinking business client who continually boasts about his ethnic background. He claims to be half Irish, a quarter German, and a quarter Italian. (Yet I know he also must be at least a fifth Scotch.)

My father-in-law dislikes talking on the telephone, especially during his leisure hours. You might say he has a hangup about phones. (You also might say that he is not a phony person.)

A member of the Board of Education in our city, who was accused of personally profiting from the sale of blackboards to the city's schools, was not supported by his own party for re-election. The party wanted to run with a clean slate.

A bachelor designed a special lock for the door of his apartment, which he controls by a button near his couch. He calls the device his pad lock.

A young man who had recently moved out of his parents' house to make it on his own in the city was ironing his own clothes one day. When he turned around for a minute to answer the phone, he burned a large hole in the seat of his best pants. "Now I really have burned my breeches behind me," he sighed.

After a mother had collected all her baby's dirty clothes to take to the laundry, the baby opened the lid of the basket and threw everything out. You might say the mother was hampered in her efforts.

As a result of forgetting to change clothes after school, a boy came home from a baseball game with a grass stain on his new pants. Upon seeing his mother, he inquired why she was looking at him with disdain. His mother angrily replied, "You're the one with the stain."

When told by his teacher that the principal demanded his presence, the smart aleck student replied, "I don't have any presents; the stores were all closed."

A friend of mine gave me a quarter cigar. He had already smoked the first three-quarters.

When the metric system becomes widespread, I assume schoolchildren will learn about the gram in grammer school. They probably will also be taught a new game called "Follow the Litre."

I'm sure that many people have not heard my pun about the pocket calculator. It figures.

If it is true that April showers bring May flowers, then what do May flowers bring? Pilgrims, I guess.

There was a fickle girl in high school named Barbara whom everyone called "Barb" for short because no one knew her very long.

I was informed that the Evanston Township High School Pun Club plans to mobilize its own police force; they are going to use punmarked cars, however.

We once attended a fund-raising dinner in a crowded banquet room, and were seated directly in front of the men's room. I told everyone we were seated at the head table.

A couple of months ago a midget who was interviewed on a television talk show made the comment that a number of midgets have a tendency to sell themselves short.

A dense fog in our area is causing a number of accidents on the highway. When the fog clears, it won't be mist.

I knew a girl a number of years ago who was as pure as Snow White; however, she has since drifted quite a bit.

I have a crazy cousin who takes an airplane trip at least once a month. You might describe her as a flighty person.

Last night I was late getting home because I got struck behind a guy driving ten miles an hour on a busy two-lane road. The guy was really a creep.

A man came into a pawn shop to hock some cultured pearls. When asked by the pawnbroker whether the pearls were really cultured, the man responded, "These pearls are so cultured that if they could talk, they wouldn't speak to either of us."

To me "investing" is spending the extra money necessary to buy a three piece suit.

A few nights ago a violent windstorm broke off a number of the shutters on our house. I shudder to think how much it will cost to replace them.

T-shirts that are imprinted with a good pun are shirts that will never be outgroaned.

This year we have a lot of crabgrass in our lawn. In fact, our grass is so crabby that when we sprinkle it, it spits water back at us.

Two men, who had met the previous day, ran into each other again at the urinals of a men's room in their hotel and had the following conversation:
Mr. Potter (V): Are you here on the American or European Plan?
Mr. Potts (P): We're here on the American Plan, but European on my shoe.

I once handled a case for a woman with seven children. I found her to be overbearing.

I understand that Lady Godiva was the biggest gambler of all time. She put everything she had on a horse.

In the Fall of 1977 I did a segment of the *Jim Beedle Show* on WAIT radio in Chicago. At first I was afraid Mr. Beedle would bug me, but I soon realized that he was a Jim-dandy guy.

It has been said that when I curtailed my law practice to write *PUNishment*, I had decided to go into pun formation.

There is no question that in recent years puns have groan in popularity.

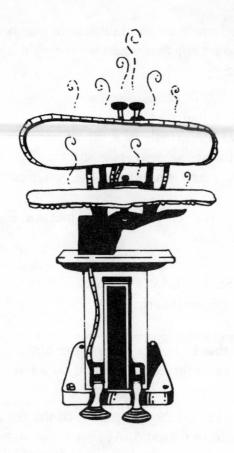

PUNishment was originally published by my own company, The Punster's Press. The printing press we used has brought us fame and fortune. Above is a picture of the world-famous Punster's Press, where we print our books and press our pants.

If I ever decide to incorporate my company, I will have to call it "The Punster's Press, Ink."

I understand that Adam and Eve were diligent sugar farmers. Whenever they were able, they were raising Cain.

When asked by his mother whether he took a bath that evening, the precocious youngster responded, "Why? Is there one missing?"

One might consider a grandfather clock to be an old timer.

In his Chicago *Daily News* column last year, fellow punster Bob Herguth pointed out that since my book was relatively clean, I could not call it *Grime and PUNishment*. (But wait for my next book.)

II MULTILINGUAL PUNS

18. INTRODUCTION

I would define a "multilingual pun" simply as a pun using the words of more than one language. In this secion I have included multilingual puns involving English and a handful of foreign languages.

The idea of establishing a multilingual category is a relatively recent one, and for that reason a great number of puns have not been accumulated in this section. I have merely tried to give a few examples from a small number of different languages to lay the groundwork for a potentially rich source of new material.

While all the puns in this section are bilingual, consisting of English and one foreign language, there is no reason why puns could not be included involving English and two or more other languages, or just two or more foreign languages. For instance, a multilingual punster could pun on the Japanese word "tora," meaning "tiger," with the Hebrew word "Torah," referring to that part of the Hebrew Bible known as the "Pentateuch" or Law of Moses. (The punster could even ask someone if he has seen that World War II movie about the Bible called Tora! Tora! Tora!) With this potentially vast source of material available to him, there is no limit to the pundemonium a multilingual punster could cause.

19. FRENCH

I was told that a Frenchman only has one egg for breakfast because one egg is an oeuf.

I know a man who has worked 40 years as a chauffeur and has nothing to show for it.

The word "connoisseur" could best describe my friend Pierre. Someone recently ran off with his girlfriend and he's kind of sore about it.

A friend of mine told me that on his last trip to Paris he met and became friendly with an attractive French girl. The night he brought her back to his hotel room he recalls her saying, "Je t'adore" over and over, and he kept replying, "It's closed, it's closed."

The luckiest hours for men in Paris are between midnight and 4:00 A.M., and are known as "the oui hours of the morning."

We met a Frenchman in Geneva who looked twenty years younger because of the toupee he was wearing. Of course, he had to pay a lot for it.

20. GERMAN

When asked, "Was ist los?" I replied. "That which has not been tied down yet."

I came back from Europe thinking German families were very large. Many times when I would ask Germans if they had any children, they would reply, "Nein."

An American businessman went into a bar in West Berlin and ordered a dry martini. When the bartender appeared to be confused, the American repeated "dry martini." The bartender shrugged and fixed the man three martinis.

At the winter Olympics games in Innsbruck, Austria, the starter for the downhill ski race would start the skiers with the following count: "Eins, zwei, drei, vier." Before his turn on a rather snowy and hazardous day, one American said to another, "We have nothing to fear but Vier itself."

21. HEBREW

Passover has sometimes been called the days of wine and chàrosis.

Passover could also have been the inspiration for the song "Seder, you with the stars in your eyes . . ." (I must apologize for this one.)

A friend of mine is writing a movie script entitled "Frontier Rabbi." The other day he was describing a scene from the script where the rabbi conducts a short mourning service in the wilderness. I told him the scene could be called "A Little Kaddish in the Woods."

When a hospital visitor asked two Jewish patients how bad their hemorrhoid operations were, they jointly replied, "It tuchas a long time to recover."

People who are in need of a babysitter will often go to a Jewish bookstore and select the siddur of their choice.

I understand that when the ex-Shah of Iran left New York, a special bus took him to the airport on a Saturday. The transportation was referred to as "the Shah-bus service."

22. SPANISH

A very special drink is made in Mexico by taking a certain kind of bird and dipping it into a glass of tequila several times. I believe the drink is called "tequila mockingbird."

When my cousin Brad was in a small village in Mexico, he became acquainted with one of the villagers who was planning to take a long journey. When Brad asked him where he was going, the man replied, "to ciudad," to which Brad responded, "You know my father?"

A few years ago I was walking down a street in a Mexican border town on an extremely hot day when I heard a voice calling out "Limonada, limonada." Recognizing a chance to try out my Spanish, I said to the vendor, "Es fria?" He replied, "No, señor. You have to pay for it."

When cowboys in South America match their skills during organized competition in steer-roping, bronco-riding, etc., they receive evaluation scores in each event; these grades are commonly referred to as "gaucho marks."

Some burglars broke into the home of a wealthy family in San Juan and stole every antique vase in the family's large and valuable collection, with the exception of one. The burglars tried to add a little humor to the situation by leaving a recording of the great Latin American favorite, "Solamente Una Vez."

At the hotel we were staying at in Acapulco a combo would play music every afternoon by the pool. The combo referred to their sunbathing songs as "sol" music.

III   THE ART OF PUNNING OR HOW TO LOSE FRIENDS AND AGONIZE PEOPLE

23. TECHNIQUES FOR PUNSTERS

If the reader has had the endurance to become familiar with the collection of puns in the first part of the book, he is now ready to develop the punning techniques which I believe separate a true artist from a person who can occasionally rattle off a pun when he hears a familiar word. Discussed below are a few basic techniques and a few secondary techniques, which will guide a punster in develping the ability to blend clever puns smoothly into normal conversation.

First of all, and of utmost importance, a punster who is verbally interacting with other people should only use puns that make sense in the context of that interaction. The mere fact that he knows a pun on a word that comes up in the conversation (or which is brought to mind by the situation) does not mean he should use it at that time unless it reasonably fits in with what is being discussed (or what is happening). A punster should strive to make his puns with a perfectly straight face, in a normal tone of voice, so that they are consistent with the rest of the conversation. When a pun is told in this manner, it is not unusual for at least one person in the group not to know what hit him until someone groans it to his attention. (If no one in the group catches the pun, be sure to stop the conversation, smile, and tell everyone what a great play on words they just missed!)

The following are some illustrations of the first

technique from my personal experiences. One night during my college days I was at a restaurant in St. Louis with some friends. We finished our main course, and I asked the waitress for the dessert menu. She replied that the only dessert left that night was rice pudding. I instantaneously responded in a disbelieving tone of voice, "You're putting me on."

There was also the time a number of years ago when my younger brother David came home from the zoo and told me he had spent a full hour in the lion house. With a straight face and without any hesitation I replied, "I think you're lion."

In my days as a law clerk in the Illinois Attorney General's Antitrust Division, my boss once told me to find a case supporting a certain point of law, which he urgently needed in 15 minutes. I found an applicable case involving Swift and Company in approximately 5 minutes. Later that day my boss was complimenting me on how well I came through in finding the Swift case. I responded with something like, "Yes, I guess I was pretty swift about it." (It turned out that for some reason I was transferred to another division a few months later.)

A couple of years ago at my old law firm I went to see the bookkeeper about getting reimbursed for some cab fares and other business expenses I had paid for out of my own money. She took out a pad of petty cash slips and had me fill out a couple. When I finished, she said, "Why don't you keep the rest of this pad for future use," to which I replied, "Great! I've always wanted a pad of my own."

Recently, I was in Kansas City on behalf of one of my clients, trying to arrange new mortgage financing for a small shopping center. While driving down a major commercial highway, one of the mortgage bankers I was with said, "Look at all the doughnut shops that are going out of business," to which I immediately replied, "Apparently, they're running out of dough." (For some reason it took an unusually long time to get a loan for that particular shopping center.)

Finally, during the last football season I was very much involved in watching the playoff games on television while my wife was wrapping Christmas gifts. She commented that she needed some ribbon for the gifts, and I promised to go out and get some at the end of the game, in about a half hour. After over an hour had passed, and the game was not over, she said something like, "I'm sure glad I have all this ribbon to wrap the presents," to which I shouted, "Quit ribbing me!"

On all of the above occasions I came up with puns that made sense in light of the remarks directed at me, and which were logical continuations of the ongoing conversations. The puns made in these situations should be contrasted with the following puns which were made by other persons in my presence: "I can't bear the thought" (by a bear exhibit at the local zoo), "That's a lot of bull" (upon seeing a bull from a car on a country road), and

"Something fishy is going on here" (upon catching a fish on a Wisconsin lake). When the above puns were made, the amateur punsters involved were merely reciting puns on easily-punable words without regard to the context of the situation; the puns were not meaningful in light of what was happening at the time, nor were they a response to something said or done by another person. An accomplished punster would not have impugned his honor with those puns.

My second technique, which potentially could be the most useful and productive, is utilized in situations where a punster thinks of or is reminded of a good pun he would like to make, but feels he cannot smoothly fit it into the ongoing conversation. In these situations a punster should create tangential conversation or concoct a plausible story that will enable him to make his pun effectively. The created conversation should flow smoothly from and be a reasonably logical extension of the ongoing conversation, and again, should be done in normal tone of voice with a perfectly straight face.

A couple of examples will help illustrate this technique. Some time ago there was a popular discount department store chain in the Chicagoland area called "Shopper's World." One time I was involved in a conversation in which someone was discussing the unpleasantness of her last visit to the dentist. I subsequently went off on a tangent that went something like this: "Speaking of dentists, I just read in the paper yesterday that they are planning to open a huge dental office on the near north side with chairs for 25 dentists. I think they intend to call the office Chopper's World."

On another occasion, I was with a group of people who were talking about their respective vacations to Europe. When it was my turn, I made up the following story: "Of all the countries in Europe, I had the best time in Finland. That's probably because I speak the language." Someone in the group then said, "You speak Finnish?" I replied, "That's right. However, I must admit that my Finnish isn't too good; but, neither is my beginning."

In both of the above situations I manipulated and altered the direction of the conversation to give myself the opportunity to slip in one of my favorite puns. My audience was not aware that my stories were complete fabrications until I lowered the boom on them. It takes years of dedicated practice to be convincing in setting up a pun in this manner without letting people know that you are not for real.

A variation on my second technique, which has given me a great deal of mileage, is picking up a newspaper or magazine and pretending to read (or summarize) some fictitious event. One time at my in-laws' house I picked up the Sunday paper, pretended to be looking at a specific news account, and said the following: "Did you see this article about the terrorists in Nicaragua?" (My in-laws indicated they had not.) "They tried to kill one of their political opponents, a matador, by planting a bomb in the stomach of one of the bulls in the ring. The whole situation is becoming abominable." (My in-laws subsequently told my wife and I that it was time for them to retire for the night.)

The third basic technique is often invoked when a punster really has to stretch the words in his pun or when the pun he plans to use is a little on the obvious side. Also, this technique can be used when the punster is not sure whether or not he has already perpetrated the pun he has in mind on the people he is with. In all these circumstances, the thing to do is to make the pun by blaming it on someone else.

I have three favorite ways of putting the blame on someone else, which once again can best be illustrated by a few examples. If the subject of Moors comes up in a discussion of history or culture, you might look at the person you're talking to at an appropriate point in the conversation and say with an acknowledging nod of the head, "I know what you're thinking: the Moor the merrier." Alternately, if you happened to be discussing great artistic painters, you might turn to someone with a grimacing look at some opportune moment and accusingly say, "You're probably going to say something like 'Easel come, easel go.' " As another possibility, when the time is right and you are talking about oil with the ideal prospective victim, you can simply say with a look of anguish, "I know. The oily bird gets the worm."

In essence, the third technique is a useful device for the times a punster is a little embarrassed or inhibited about making a particular pun, and a suitable scapegoat is present. In addition, this technique affords one the unique opportunity of being a punster at the same time he is pretending to react like one of the unfortunate victims.

It should be pointed out at this time that there are occasions when the people you are with really do inadvertently make puns. As the enlightened punster, you have the option of either pointing out and complimenting the person on his pun, or letting him know about it with a look and words of anguish, depending on who the unenlightened punster is and the circumstances involved. I recall one particular lecture in my commercial law class at Northwestern University when our professor was discussing a particular case dealing with a swimming pool company. During the discussion, the professor made comments about how the business had "liquidity" problems that eventually forced the owner "to go under," and when the bank that had loaned him money took over, they were anxious to "wash their hands of the business." Considering who was involved and the circumstances, I definitely felt it was in my best interests to compliment the professor on his subtle punmanship.

When the circumstances that would occasion the use of my third technique exist, but it might be difficult or awkward to imply that a particular pun is on someone else's mind, a punster should use my fourth basic technique. The fourth technique is actually a tactful way of coping with the moments of weakness that every punster occasionally has when he feels that he absolutely has to make a certain pun or his mind will not be at ease. If you are the punster when these circumstances occur, the following approach should be taken. At some appropriate point in the conversation, you should make your pun in a very deliberate manner by giving the impression that everyone knows the pun should be said, and it might as well be you who gets the job done. For instance, if the subject again happens to be oil (and assuming you have the courage), you could use expressions like, "You know the old saying—'Oil's fair in love and war,'" or, "You know what they always say—'Oil's well that ends well.'" It should be pointed out, however, that even when this technique and the third one are used, the puns must be reasonably consistent with the context of the conversation and situation, lest the punster lower himself to the level of a mere amateur.

Initially, a punster is likely to use the basic techniques discussed above with adaptable puns he has absorbed and stored in his mind for future reference. Hopefully, however, he will eventually start to think like a veteran punster and develop the ability to create new puns spontaneously while involved in ordinary conversation.

In addition to my basic techniques, there are a few secondary techniques which can be used by a person who has already started to think like a seasoned punster and whose ears are attuned to hearing punable words. The secondary techniques are more limited in applicability because their use is more dependent on the specific words of others. Nevertheless, these methods of punning have been used most effectively by some well-known people in the world of comedy, and can offer a talented punster additional excellent ways of PUNishing his victims.

There are occasions when someone will say a word that reminds you of a similar-sounding word. In these situations the punster can pretend that he did not hear what the person said, and inquire whether the person said the word the punster is thinking of. A couple of examples again will best illustrate this technique.

A number of years ago my younger brother Marc came home from a barber shop in Winnetka, Illinois, and my grandfather Jake said to him, "Say, that's a nice haircut. Where did you get it?" My brother replied, "At Smales," to which my grandfather responded, "What! You say it smells?"

On another occasion, my wife and I were dining at a restaurant in Florida. The waiter asked my wife what kind of potatoes she wanted with her meal—mashed or au gratin. I quickly interjected, "You say your potatoes are rotten?"

There was also the time at one of my summer jobs during college when my supervisor and I were discussing a cost-benefit study we were planning to make for a new highway project. My supervisor said something like, "I have very distinct ideas about how to structure this study," to which I quickly responded, "You say your ideas stink?" (It so happens that I was not rehired by that company the following summer.)

To use this type of punning, the people you are

with must cooperate by saying the right words; also the punster must have sharp ears and enough punning experience to recognize special words which could spontaneously be turned into questioning puns. (Groucho Marx made extremely humorous use of this method of punning on his *You Bet Your Life* show.)

Closely related to the above technique are the corollary techniques of responding to a punable word said by another person by knowingly continuing the conversation in a direction not intended by the victim (until you pretend to acknowledge your minunderstanding at some point), or by physically reacting to what is said in a manner not anticipated by the victim. Again, a few personal experiences can best demonstrate what I have in mind.

A few years ago, I was shopping for some furniture for my apartment with my girlfriend. At one store, I was talking to a salesman about end tables. The salesman looked at one particular table, which was situated next to my girlfriend, and said, "There's a real beauty. Just look at those legs." I continued to look in the direction of the table and my girlfriend and said something like this, "Yes, those are nice legs. And look at the rest of that body, and those sexy eyes," I slowly turned toward the salesman's puzzled face, hesitated, and then said with a look of sudden enlightenment, "Oh! You mean the table! I thought you meant the young lady." The salesman managed to fake a faint smile and a slight laugh, and politely suggested that I look around the store on my own for a while.

More recently, when I first started working for a law firm, a secretary in the firm and I had a discussion about the work habits of the various lawyers in the office. At one point in the discussion she was talking about how sloppy and disorganized the senior partner's office was, referring to the ever-present foot-high layer of papers on his desk. She subsequently asked me if I kept my drawers neat, to which I replied, "Oh, yes. My wife irons and folds every pair." After hearing her snicker a few seconds later, I pretended to see the light by saying, "Oh, you mean my desk drawers. Yes, they're pretty neat." (Bob Cummings made extensive use of this type of humor on his *Love That Bob* show.)

Turning to the second variation, I recall the time a number of months ago when my wife and I were having dinner at a well-known restaurant in Chicago. My wife had ordered trout and I had ordered roast duck. The waiter brought out my wife's dinner and a short time later the captain came out of the kitchen with my roast duck. He approached our table and said in a questioning tone, "Duck?" I instantly ducked my head beneath the table (with my arm over my head), to the total bafflement of the captain, the embarrassment of my wife and the amusement of the couple at the next table. After the captain stood in silence for a few seconds, my wife said to him, "Yes, he ordered duck," at which point the man put my dinner down with a slight, forced smile and left. It so happened that upon leaving the restaurant, instead of hearing the usual "Good night, please come again," all we heard was "Good night." (The Marx Brothers made excellent use of this form of punmanship in their many movies.)

As a final example of the above two corollary techniques I recall a very recent incident which demonstrates how the two methods of punning can be combined effectively. My wife and I went to a restaurant in a nearby suburb with my cousin Harley. As we walked in the door, the hostess came up to greet us and said to my cousin, "Check your coat?" Harley immediately proceeded to examine every inch of his coat from top to bottom, then turned to the bewildered hostess and said, "Looks all right to me." (The great Mel Brooks has hilariously combined the two techniques (and used each separately) in his recent movies and personal interviews.)

As with the mishearing technique initially discussed, the misunderstanding and physical reaction techniques require the victim to provide the punster with the right words to play off, and the punster must be able to react spontaneously. These two methods of punning are especially suited to those readers with a flair for the dramatic.

Finally, there are occasional opportunities when a punster can conspire with others and engage in premeditated PUNishment. This method can be used if there is a person present who is familiar with the development of a particular pun or if a specific routine can be prearranged. For example, a number of my friends are familiar with the "weak back" pun so that on any given occasion the following dialogue might take place:

Punster: Boy, my back is really bothering me.

Victim: What's wrong with it?

Punster: I don't know. I guess I just have a weak back.

Conspirator: When did you get it?

Punster: Oh, about a week back.

It should be remembered that when punsters conspire to perpetrate puns like this, their puns must still be blended smoothly into the ongoing conversation either by cleverly fitting them into whatever is being discussed, or by creating tangential conversation which sets up the opportunity to insert them.

In connection with premeditated PUNishment, a word should be said about punning by public speakers. A person giving a speech has virtually complete control over what he says and therefore could have clever puns planned for appropriate points in his speech. With the ability to prepare or at least structure what he is going to say in advance, there is no reason why the public speaker's puns should not be blended into his speech in the smoothest possible manner.

When the reader has thoroughly familiarized himself with a number of the puns in the first part of the book and understands the punning techniques outlined above, he is ready to be unleashed upon the public. Hopefully, the categorical collection and the suggested techniques will serve as a training manual until the art becomes second nature.

Before starting out to inflict PUNishment on unsuspecting victims, the prospective punster must be sure that he has a sufficient quantity of friends in case some get lost along the way. He also must be aware that the art of punning is potentially a most powerful weapon that should be used with great caution and discretion. With all this in mind, it's now time for the punster to start losing friends and agonizing people.

24. FURTHERANCE OF THE ART

In this book I have tried to lay two foundations. The first is the beginning of a categorical collection of puns, and the second is hopefully a starting point for a guide to the art of punning. I would like to build up both of these foundations in the future. It is my hope that subsequent editions of *PUNishment* will incorporate a much larger number of puns, as well as additional punning techniques and ideas for the furtherance of the art.

I would also like to see recognition given for the best puns made spontaneously in normal conversation and for the best original puns per se. Possibly this acknowledgment could be accomplished through a future national or international association of punsters dedicated to the art of punning.* In addition, I think live competition in punning could be organized someday. Either individual punsters or teams of punsters could square off in five-minute rounds on designated subject matter with a group of judges deciding who demonstrated the greatest punning ability.

It is my hope that *PUNishment* will in some way help gain recognition for, and inspire contributions to, the noble art of punning. I have two basic reasons for wanting this increased recognition and wider acceptance. First, recognition is long overdue for the pun as an important and basic form of humor. Second, and more important, is the

---

I wish to express my gratitude to fellow punsters around the world who have shared their interest in punning and who have expressed enthusiasm for the furtherance of the art.

fact that I am greatly concerned about the possibility that *PUNishment* will be considered cruel and unusual punishment in violation of the Eighth Amendment to the Constitution of the United States. The exact language of the Eighth Amendment, which is part of the Bill of Rights, is as follows:

> Excessive bail shall not be required, nor excessive fines imposed, nor cruel and unusual punishments inflicted. (Emphasis added)

The language of this amendment has been interpreted by the courts of the land to mean that a form of punishment must be both cruel and unusual to be prohibited.

It would be extremely difficult to argue that *PUNishment* is not cruel, for its main purpose is to develop and promulgate the art of punning, and a punster who masters the art is bound to lose friends and agonize people. The only chance the book has of not falling within the scope of the Eighth Amendment is for the art to become a more usual form of punishment. In other words, the art of punning must be widely accepted and recognized as a form of punishment in order for *PUNishment* not to be prohibited as cruel and unusual punishment.

As I am about to finish writing this book, I have already received the following communications:

— Telegrams from a number of kings and queens around the world, asking me to acknowledge their respective "royalty" rights.

— Letters of concern from the Chamber of Commerce of Miami Beach, Florida, that if I moved to their city, there would be a danger that the nickname for Miami Beach might be changed to "The Sun and Pun Capital of the World."

— And phone calls from various philanthropic and humanitarian organizations offering to send me (as soon as possible) on an all-expense-paid trip of indefinite duration to Antarctica and points south. (Isle sea you there)

EPILOGUE

When things get rough and
you cannot seem to gain any ground,
drop back and

PUN.